D0833916

TV COOKS

Antonio Carluccio

COOKS

Pasta

BBC

Published by BBC Worldwide Limited,
Woodlands, 80 Wood Lane,
London W12 0TT

The recipes in this book first appeared in
Antonio Carluccio's Passion for Pasta
© Antonio Carluccio 1993

This edition first published 1999
© Antonio Carluccio 1999
The moral right of the author has been asserted

ISBN 0 563 38455 7

Photographs: Juliet Piddington
© BBC Worldwide Limited 1999

Project Editor: Charlotte Lochhead
Editor: Pam Mallender
Design: Town Group Creative
Stylist and Home Economist:
Sarah Ramsbottom
Author Photograph: Graham Kirk

Set in New Caledonia and Helvetica
Printed and bound in France by
Imprimerie Pollina S.A., Luçon, France
Colour separations by
Imprimerie Pollina S.A.
Cover printed by Imprimerie Pollina S.A.

Cover and frontispiece:
Penne with Chilli Sauce

CONTENTS

Recipe Notes &
  Handy Conversion Tables   **4**

Introduction by Antonio Carluccio   **5**

Ingredients & Equipment Glossary   **6**

Ingredients   **8**

Equipment   **10**

Soups   **12**

Pasta with Meat   **16**

Pasta with Fish   **24**

Vegetarian Pasta   **32**

Baked Dishes   **43**

Pasta Salads   **52**

Pasta Desserts   **56**

Basics   **60**

Index   **63**

RECIPE NOTES

Wash all fresh produce before preparation and peel as necessary.

Spoon measurements are level. Always use proper measuring spoons: 1 teaspoon = 5ml and 1 tablespoon = 15ml.

Never mix metric and imperial measures in one recipe. Stick to one or the other.

Nutritional notes are for a single serving, when the dish is made for the number of servings stated in the recipe (unless indicated otherwise).

Eggs are medium. If your kitchen is warm, keep the eggs in the fridge, but allow them to come to room temperature before using. While the proven risks of healthy people becoming ill from eating fresh raw eggs are minimal, pregnant women, the sick, the elderly and the very young should avoid eating raw or partially cooked eggs.

HANDY CONVERSION TABLES

Weight		Volume		Linear	
15g	½oz	30ml	1fl oz	5mm	¼in
25g	1oz	50ml	2fl oz	10mm/1cm	⅛in
40g	1½oz	100ml	3½fl oz	2cm	¾in
55g	2oz	125ml	4fl oz	2.5cm	1in
85g	3oz	150ml	5fl oz (¼ pint)	5cm	2in
115g	4oz	175ml	6fl oz	7.5cm	3in
140g	5oz	200ml	7fl oz (⅓ pint)	10cm	4in
175g	6oz	225ml	8fl oz	13cm	5in
200g	7oz	250ml	9fl oz	15cm	6in
225g	8oz	300ml	10fl oz (½ pint)	18cm	7in
250g	9oz	350ml	12fl oz	20cm	8in
280g	10oz	400ml	14fl oz	23cm	9in
350g	12oz	425ml	15fl oz (¾ pint)	25cm	10in
375g	13oz	450ml	16fl oz	28cm	11in
400g	14oz	500ml	18fl oz	30cm	12in
425g	15oz	600ml	20fl oz (1 pint)		
450g	1lb	700ml	1¼ pints	**Oven Temperatures**	
550g	1¼lb	850ml	1½ pints	110C 225F GAS ¼	
750g	1lb 10oz	1 litre	1¾ pints	120C 250F GAS ½	
900g	2lb	1.2 litres	2 pints	140C 275F GAS 1	
1kg	2¼lb	1.3 litres	2¼ pints	150C 300F GAS 2	
1.3kg	3lb	1.4 litres	2½ pints	160C 325F GAS 3	
1.8kg	4lb	1.7 litres	3 pints	180C 350F GAS 4	
2.25kg	5lb	2 litres	3½ pints	190C 375F GAS 5	
		2.5 litres	4½ pints	200C 400F GAS 6	
				220C 425F GAS 7	
				230C 450F GAS 8	
				240C 475F GAS 9	

Ⓥ   **Suitable for vegetarians**

Pasta, in any shape or form, is probably one of the most popular dishes eaten worldwide. It is extremely simple to prepare and immensely rewarding to eat provided it is cooked properly. The preparation of a perfect plate of pasta requires some basic culinary knowledge, a little patience and a great deal of love and dedication. Once you have learnt the basics of pasta making and cooking, using this book, you will get huge satisfaction in eating what is one of the healthiest and most wholesome of foods.

It is always very interesting to watch the faces of guests after they have tasted a morsel of juicy, well cooked and well dressed pasta. The resulting contented smile is always a reward for the cook's labours. It is enough to watch the expression of a small child sucking on a string of spaghetti or tagliatelle to guess how much pleasure is derived by this funny food, even at a tender young age.

In fact, I have had my passion for pasta since I was a child. I was brought up in a family of six children and, although pasta is served with other dishes as part of a typical Italian meal, it was always my favourite one. My mother had the important task of producing many different pasta dishes to give us daily variety, and boy she was good at it! All through the morning at school we used to think with anticipation of the steamy plate of pasta waiting for us at the table on our return. Many of my mother's dishes are reproduced in this book, which is based on my *Passion for Pasta* book. They have been selected by the BBC as the most delicious recipes that you might like to try. I hope you enjoy them and I wish you *Buon Appetito!*

INGREDIENTS

Basil

This is without doubt the king of herbs in Italian cookery. Orginally coming from India, via Arabia, to the south of Italy, enthusiasm for its use spread over the rest of Europe, and now basil is one of the most favoured herbs. Only fresh basil leaves produce that wonderful, sweet scent we all know. The dried ones taste completely different. Nowadays it is possible to grow basil through the winter too, so there need not be any temptation to use the dried variety. If you can't get fresh basil, the famous Pesto *alla Genovese* may be the solution. Pesto is a sauce originally made from a very small-leaved variety of basil, grown along the Ligurian Riviera.

Cheese

In Italy we say *'Come il cacio sui maccheroni'* (Like cheese on pasta) to describe two things which are so appropriate together they become virtually inseparable. Pasta without a sprinkling of freshly grated Parmesan cheese is almost unthinkable. There are, however, dishes where cheese is taboo, such as when pasta has a fish sauce.

Parmesan: only cheese made in the region of Reggio Emilia is able to carry the name *Parmigiano reggiano* (the full, registered name for Parmesan). It is made with cow's milk and is very low in fat (only 30 per cent) but has a particularly fine smell and taste. It should have a very grainy texture, without smelling 'cheesy' at all. It is usually at least 14 months old and pale yellow. Buy a wedge, wrap it in foil and it will keep in the fridge for several weeks. Avoid drums and sachets of ready grated Parmesan – they never taste like the fresh cheese.

Pecorino: the three best-known varieties of this sheep's milk cheese come from the regions of Lazio (*Pecorino Romano*); Sardinia (*Pecorino Sardo*) and Tuscany (*Pecorino Toscano*). Everywhere in southern Italy Pecorino is often used in place of Parmesan cheese. It is a quick-maturing cheese and is excellent fresh and grated. Mature Pecorino is almost as hard as Parmesan cheese in texture, and gives certain recipes an extra 'bite'.

Ricotta: this is a low-fat, soft cheese, similar to cottage cheese, but is not at all sour. If ricotta has any hint of acidity then it is 'off'. It can be made from goat's, sheep's or cow's milk.

Dried mushrooms

So beloved are dried, wild mushrooms to me that I keep many varieties in my larder and I would encourage you to keep at least the ceps and morels.

Ceps: called *porcini* in Italy, these have a very distinctive, concentrated flavour, almost like meat extract, so it is enough to use them in small quantities. Just 25g/1oz dried ceps will make all the difference to a sauce containing 450g/1lb fresh mushrooms.

Morels: these are the most expensive wild mushroom. They have a very intensive flavour, almost like bacon, and are usually only available whole.

Dried pasta

Dried pasta can taste as heavenly as fresh if it is well prepared, and accompanied by the right sauce. It is available with and without eggs. Pasta *secca all'uovo*, dried egg pasta, is very brittle in its uncooked state while pasta *secca,* made from durum-wheat semolina and water, with no addition of eggs or other ingredients, is by far the most widely used pasta in Italy, because it is more economical. As the dough is easier to work with than an egg pasta it can produce an enormous variety of shapes. And the pleasure of eating the right combination of texture, shape and flavour is taken very seriously. Altogether the Italians have invented more that 300 different shapes; each one suitable for a certain sauce. So it is not surpising that they are not always labelled by the same name commercially. But don't be put off by the choice – the variety makes for so much fun. Generally speaking, anything with the word *rigate* after it is ridged, and anything called *lisce* is smooth. (See page 60 for notes on fresh pasta and cooking al dente.)

Pancetta

This is the Italian equivalent of bacon and is used a great deal in Italy in the same way streaky bacon is used here. It comes in two shapes, rolled or flat, and has been air-cured with the addition of some spices. I suggest you buy it in slices rather than a whole piece. If you can't find it use bacon.

Parma ham

Perhaps surprisingly, it is the fat of Parma ham which is especially useful for sauces and soups. You may find you can buy just the end of a Parma ham from your delicatessen. It will be cheaper than buying slices from the main part of the ham and very useful when fried in small cubes to add flavour to a recipe.

Salt and pepper

It helps to have salt in two forms; coarse and fine, and it should be sea salt. Add salt to the boiling water just before the pasta. Use coarse sea salt and in the ratio of one teaspoon per 1 litre/1¾ pints of water. You need 1 litre/1¾ pints of water per 115g/4oz of pasta being cooked. Whole black peppercorns, freshly ground, taste infinitely better than ready ground pepper.

Truffles

For me, the only form in which to use truffle is fresh. This very expensive commodity is available only between October and January. Naturally I'm talking about the white truffle from around Alba in Piedmont. Truffle is a fungus that grows under the earth and can't be cultivated. If you want a real treat, then buy a small one. A 15g/½oz serving per person is sufficient. The black truffle, as found in Umbria in Italy and Perigord in France, is used mainly for cooking but is not intense enough to flavour the whole dish.

EQUIPMENT

Pans

You do need a large stainless steel saucepan for cooking pasta. Ideally it should be shaped so it is wide at the bottom to keep the temperature of the water constant. Special pasta pans, which have a removable container in which the pasta sits and cooks, are also very useful. Most of the cooking water drains straight back into the pan as you remove the pasta holder, so there is no need for a large colander. A few of the recipes ask you to cook the sauce for quite a time, so check that your pan for sauce has a heavy base.

Pasta machines

I am not a fan of electric pasta-mixing machines. The simplest, hand-turned rolling machines will help you, though, but everything can also be done by hand equally as well. The rolling machines come with various settings to take the work out of rolling out the pasta and have special cutters for producing different widths.

Pastry cutting wheel

This will be useful for some of the shapes. Specialist shops often sell ravioli wheels which will do instead, or buy a *raviolatrice* which is a flat, aluminium grid with cavities for producing ravioli. Make sure, though, that you have a rolling pin.

1	Capers
2	Sun dried tomatoes
3	Salted anchovies
4	Truffle (summer)
5	Basil
6	Flatleaf parsley
7	Marjoram
8	Mozzarella
9	Smoked mozzarella
10	Ricotta
11	Fontina
12	Pecorino (mature)
13	Pecorino (mild)
14	Parmesan
15	Pancetta
16	Speck
17	Parma ham
18	Morels
19	Oyster mushrooms
20	Shiitake mushrooms
21	Ceps/porcini
22	Chanterelles
23	Fresh lasagne
24	Fresh tagliatelle/fettuccine
25	Fresh angel's hair pasta
26	Fresh tagliolini
27	Fresh cappelletti
28	Fresh raviolini
29	Fresh spaghetti (square)
30	Dried penne rigate
31	Dried orecchiette
32	Dried pappardelle
33	Dried penne lisce
34	Dried tubettini
35	Dried tagliatelle/fettuccine

1. Stainless steel pasta strainer
2. Stainless steel pasta pan
3. Stainless steel pasta spoon for long pasta
4. Heavy-based frying pan
5. Cheese grater
6. Wooden pasta spoons for long pasta
7. *Forchettoni* for serving pasta
8. Pestle and mortar
9. Pepper grinder
10. Hand-turned pasta rolling machine
11. Rolling pin
12. *Raviolatrice*
13. Ravioli wheel
14. Nutmeg grater

Soups

MINESTRONE

There are many different varieties of minestrone, each one varying according to regional customs. Minestrone 'big soup' is usually prepared with leftover fresh vegetables such as peas, shredded cabbage and courgettes. I'll allow you to substitute a stock cube for home-made stock in this recipe; but only if you really have to! Depending on quantities and proportions of ingredients, minestrone can also be served as a main course. This soup makes an excellent vegetarian recipe if the meat is left out.

Serves 4

3 tbsp olive oil

1 onion, chopped

1 small garlic clove, chopped

2 rashers rindless streaky bacon, finely chopped or 25g/1oz Parma ham, finely chopped (optional)

4 celery sticks, diced

1 tomato, skinned, seeded and finely chopped

1 large carrot, diced

2 potatoes, diced

a few fresh basil leaves or 1 tbsp Pesto sauce (See Tip)

850ml/1½ pints Chicken stock (page 62)

sea salt and freshly ground black pepper

375g/13oz can borlotti beans, drained

115g/4oz dried tubettini or any short pasta

85g/3oz freshly grated Parmesan cheese

1 Heat the oil and fry the onion and garlic with the chopped bacon or Parma ham, until soft. Add the remaining vegetables, the basil or pesto, and toss well with the oil. Add the stock and bring to the boil. Reduce the heat and simmer for 10 minutes.

2 Add salt and pepper to taste and stir in the borlotti beans and the pasta. Cook for about 10 minutes or until al dente. Serve sprinkled with Parmesan cheese.

Nutrition notes per serving: *408 Calories, Protein 20g, Carbohydrate 47g, Fat 17g, Saturated fat 6g, Fibre 7g, Added sugar 0g, Salt 1.81g.*

TIP

For the Pesto sauce: place two roughly chopped garlic cloves, 40g/1½oz fresh basil leaves and 25g/1oz of pine nuts in a mortar. Add half a teaspoon of coarse sea salt and with the pestle grind, rather than pound, the ingredients using the coarseness of the salt to break them down. Gradually add 85g/3oz of freshly grated Parmesan cheese or mature Pecorino cheese and continue to work the ingredients to a pulp. Now, very slowly, add up to six tablespoons of olive oil in a steady stream and, using the pestle, incorporate just enough to achieve a smooth green sauce.

PASTA WITH PEAS

Serves 4

3 tbsp olive oil

1 small onion, finely sliced

55g/2oz cooked ham, cut into very thin strips

300g/10½oz fresh or frozen garden peas

1.2 litres/2 pints Chicken stock (page 62)

200g/7oz dried lasagne or pappardelle, broken into pieces

6 basil leaves, chopped

sea salt and freshly ground black pepper

1 Heat the oil and fry the onion until soft, then add the ham, the peas and the stock and cook for 10 minutes or until the peas are tender.

2 Add the pasta and the basil, taste, add salt and pepper and cook for 10 minutes or until the pasta is soft.

Nutrition notes per serving: 342 Calories, Protein 15g, Carbohydrate 48g, Fat 11g, Saturated fat 2g, Fibre 5g, Added sugar 0g, Salt 1.68g.

SOUP WITH CAPPELLETTI

Serves 4

1.2 litres/2 pints Chicken stock (page 62)

1 ripe tomato, skinned, seeded and finely chopped

140g/5oz cappelletti or raviolini (See Tip)

sea salt and freshly ground black pepper

25g/1oz freshly grated Parmesan cheese and 2 tsp coarsely chopped celery or a few leaves flatleaf parsley, to serve

1 Bring the stock to the boil, add the tomato and cook for a few minutes. Add the pasta and simmer for 7–12 minutes until al dente. Check seasoning and serve sprinkled with the Parmesan cheese and either the celery or parsley.

Nutrition notes per serving: 171 Calories, Protein 8g, Carbohydrate 29g, Fat 3g, Saturated fat 1g, Fibre 1g, Added sugar 0g, Salt 1.42g.

TIP

You'll find it easier to use dried pasta for this recipe, rather than making your own. However, if you do decide to make your own (page 60) or you manage to find some fresh cappelletti or raviolini, use 250g/9oz and cook for 5–7 minutes.

Meat

TAGLIATELLE WITH CHICKEN LIVERS

Serves 4

300g/10½oz chicken livers, thawed if frozen (See Tip, page 48)

6 tbsp olive oil

1 large onion, very finely sliced

4 bay leaves

pinch of freshly grated nutmeg

3 tbsp dry sherry

2 tbsp tomato purée

2 tbsp Chicken stock (page 62) or water

sea salt and freshly ground black pepper

450g/1lb fresh tagliatelle (page 60)

85g/3oz freshly grated Pecorino cheese

1 Cut the chicken livers into small slivers. Heat the oil and fry the onion very gently for 5 minutes until softened but not coloured. Add the chicken livers and bay leaves and fry gently for 6 minutes over a low heat.

2 Add the nutmeg and sherry, and let the alcohol evaporate for 1–2 minutes. Stir in the tomato purée and enough stock or water to bring the sauce to a smooth consistency. Season to taste with salt and pepper. Remove the bay leaves.

3 Meanwhile, cook the pasta in boiling salted water for 3–5 minutes or until al dente. Drain, then toss well in the sauce. Serve sprinkled with the Pecorino cheese.

Nutrition notes per serving: *634 Calories, Protein 35g, Carbohydrate 55g, Fat 31g, Saturated fat 9g, Fibre 4g, Added sugar trace, Salt 1.08g.*

TAGLIATELLE VERDI WITH FIELD MUSHROOMS

Serves 4

6 tbsp olive oil

2 garlic cloves, finely sliced

300g/10½oz field or button mushrooms, roughly sliced (See Tip)

4 tbsp dry white wine

115g/4oz rindless speck with fat or rindless smoked bacon, cut into strips

sea salt and freshly ground black pepper

450g/1lb fresh green tagliatelle (page 60)

85g/3oz freshly grated Parmesan cheese

4 tbsp finely chopped fresh parsley

1 Heat the oil and sweat the garlic for a few minutes. Add the mushrooms and fry over a low heat to extract their moisture. Pour in the wine and let it evaporate for 1–2 minutes. Add the speck and season to taste with salt and pepper. Cook for a few minutes until the speck browns.

2 Cook the pasta in boiling salted water for 3–5 minutes or until al dente. Drain, then toss in the sauce. Serve sprinkled with the Parmesan cheese and parsley.

Nutrition notes per serving: *641 Calories, Protein 26g, Carbohydrate 51g, Fat 37g, Saturated fat 12g, Fibre 5g, Added sugar 0g, Salt 1.96g.*

TIP

This recipe is dedicated to all those mushroom gatherers who safely collect the well-known field variety, *Agaricus bisporus*, which grows on most fields in Britain, and is related to the cultivated button mushroom. Naturally this dish tastes better with the wild, field variety but you can substitute the cultivated one.

ORECCHIETTE WITH BROCCOLI

Serves 4

450g/1lb fresh or frozen broccoli

6 tbsp olive oil

85g/3oz speck or rindless lean smoked bacon, cut into small strips

2 garlic cloves, finely chopped

300ml/½ pint milk

450g/1lb fresh orecchiette (page 60 and See Tip)

55g/2oz freshly grated Parmesan cheese

sea salt and freshly ground black pepper

1   Cook the broccoli in boiling salted water until tender. Drain well and chop very finely. Heat the oil and fry the speck or bacon until brown. Add the garlic and cook for 1 minute. Add the broccoli and season, then stir in the milk. Cook the sauce, stirring, until smooth.

2   Meanwhile, cook the pasta in boiling salted water for 6 minutes or until al dente. Drain and add to the sauce. Toss well with the Parmesan cheese, add a few grindings of black pepper and serve.

Nutrition notes per serving: *698 Calories, Protein 28g, Carbohydrate 64g, Fat 38g, Saturated fat 12g, Fibre 5g, Added sugar 0g, Salt 1.95g.*

TIP

This home-made pasta is so good that it is well worth making extra and freezing some. Although fresh, these shapes take a little longer to cook than you might expect. You can buy ready-made dried orecchiette from delicatessens. They will need to be cooked for 15–18 minutes.

PAPPARDELLE WITH MEAT SAUCE

Serves 4

6 tbsp olive oil

1 small onion, finely chopped

1 celery stick, finely chopped

1 carrot, finely chopped

200g/7oz minced pork or use 100% pork sausages, skinned

200g/7oz lean minced beef

150ml/¼ pint dry red wine

3 tbsp tomato purée diluted with 2 tbsp warm water

2 bay leaves

150ml/¼ pint Chicken stock (page 62)

sea salt and freshly ground black pepper

450g/1lb fresh pappardelle (page 60)

85g/3oz freshly grated Parmesan cheese

1   Heat the oil and gently fry the onion, celery and carrot until soft. Add the pork and beef and continue frying until the meat is browned. Pour in the wine and let it evaporate for 1–2 minutes. Add the diluted tomato purée and the bay leaves. Cook for 10 minutes.

2   Stir in the stock, add salt and pepper to taste, and then heat through for 1–2 minutes until hot. Remove the bay leaves.

3   Meanwhile, cook the pasta in boiling salted water for 5–7 minutes or until al dente. Drain and serve with the meat sauce, then sprinkle with the Parmesan cheese.

Nutrition notes per serving: *738 Calories, Protein 42g, Carbohydrate 63g, Fat 35g, Saturated fat 10g, Fibre 4g, Added sugar 0g, Salt 1.63g.*

PENNE RIGATE WITH SAUSAGE

Serves 4

Serves 4

85g/3oz butter

1 small onion, chopped

1 garlic clove, finely chopped

300g/10½oz pork sausage meat or sausages (luganega type: with a high percentage of lean pork meat)

1 fresh rosemary sprig, finely chopped

150ml/¼ pint dry white wine

pinch of freshly grated nutmeg

pinch of ground cloves

sea salt and freshly ground black pepper

375g/13oz dried penne rigate

85g/3oz freshly grated Parmesan cheese

1   Heat the butter and gently fry the onion and the garlic until softened. If using sausages, remove the skin. Break up the sausage meat with fork. Add to the pan and gently fry until well browned.

2   Add the rosemary and the wine and cook slowly for 10 minutes. Add the nutmeg, cloves and salt and pepper to taste.

3   Meanwhile, cook the pasta in boiling salted water for 7–8 minutes or until al dente, then drain. Mix with the sausage-meat mixture and add the Parmesan cheese.

Nutrition notes per serving: *889 Calories, Protein 28g, Carbohydrate 80g, Fat 50g, Saturated fat 25g, Fibre 4g, Added sugar 0g, Salt 2.72g.*

BUCATINI WITH BACON, CHEESE AND EGGS

Serves 4

400g/14oz dried bucatini (See Tip)

55g/2oz butter or 6 tbsp olive oil

115g/4oz pancetta or rindless smoked bacon, cut into small chunks

4 egg yolks

1 tbsp milk

40g/1½oz freshly grated mature Pecorino cheese

freshly ground black pepper

1   Cook the pasta in boiling salted water for 7–8 minutes or until al dente, then drain well and return to the pan and cover.

2   Heat the butter or oil and fry the pancetta or bacon until lightly browned, then set aside. Lightly beat the egg yolks and the milk together in a bowl. Add the pasta to the pancetta or bacon in the pan, pour in the egg mixture and toss together. Transfer to warm serving plates, sprinkle over the Pecorino cheese and grind over plenty of black pepper.

Nutrition notes per serving: *677 Calories, Protein 23g, Carbohydrate 76g, Fat 33g, Saturated fat 16g, Fibre 3g, Added sugar 0g, Salt 1.43g.*

TIP

Bucatini are also known as perciatelli and are like spaghetti, but with a hollow centre. In the Lazio region, surrounding Rome, bucatini is used more often than spaghetti with this sauce. Pancetta, or air-cured bacon, helps produce the authentic flavour but you can substitute green or smoked bacon, although the result is a little different.

CAUTION! This recipe contains lightly cooked eggs.

RIGATONI WITH PORK RAGOUT

Serves 4

8 tbsp olive oil

400g/14oz pork with bone such as neck, shoulder, chops or spare ribs

1 onion, finely sliced

150ml/¼ pint dry white wine

800g creamed or pulped tomatoes

2 tbsp tomato purée

2 basil leaves, chopped

sea salt and freshly ground black pepper

375g/13oz dried rigatoni

85g/3oz freshly grated Parmesan cheese

1 Heat the oil in a heavy-based pan, add the meat and fry for several minutes until browned. Add the onion and fry until golden. Pour in the wine and let it evaporate for 2 minutes.

2 Add the tomatoes and the tomato purée, cover and simmer very gently for 30 minutes. Stir the contents from time to time. Add the basil, salt and pepper to taste, and cook for another 30 minutes. If the sauce becomes too dry, add a little water.

3 Cook the pasta in boiling salted water for 8–9 minutes or until al dente, then drain. Mix the pasta with some of the sauce and serve with the remaining meat and sauce, and plenty of Parmesan cheese.

Nutrition notes per serving: *971 Calories, Protein 38g, Carbohydrate 87g, Fat 52g, Saturated fat 16g, Fibre 5g, Added sugar 6g, Salt 2.07g.*

TAGLIERINI WITH THREE MUSHROOMS

Serves 4

85g/3oz butter

1 small onion, finely chopped

55g/2oz Parma ham, finely chopped

115g/4oz fresh chanterelles, sliced

115g/4oz fresh morels, sliced

115g/4oz fresh ceps, sliced

sea salt

300g/10½oz fresh taglierini (page 60)

freshly ground black pepper

85g/3oz freshly grated Parmesan cheese

1 Heat the butter and fry the onion until golden. Add the Parma ham, fry for a few minutes, then add the mushrooms and a little salt and cook for a few minutes until the mushrooms are just softening.

2 Cook the pasta in boiling salted water for 20 seconds then drain, reserving one to two tablespoons of the cooking water. Toss the pasta with the mushrooms and a little of the cooking water to just moisten and add salt and pepper to taste. Sprinkle with Parmesan cheese to serve.

Nutrition notes per serving: *505 Calories, Protein 22g, Carbohydrate 41g, Fat 29g, Saturated fat 17g, Fibre 2g, Added sugar 0g, Salt 2.22g.*

TIP

Fresh chanterelles and morels are in season during the spring and early summer and are now available in most large supermarkets. Fresh ceps are available from August until late October. If you can't find the fresh variety, I suggest you use 25g/1oz each of any two of the mushrooms in their dried form and add 115g/4oz cultivated oyster mushrooms (or even button mushrooms) for freshness. If you do this you will need to soak the dried mushrooms in warm water for 20 minutes. Drain, squeeze dry and chop before adding to the pan.

Fish

LINGUINE WITH TUNA FISH SAUCE

The flat, slightly rounded shape of this pasta particularly suits sauces based on fish. This recipe goes to show you how useful it is to keep a tin of tuna in the cupboard.

Serves 4

4 tbsp virgin olive oil

2 garlic cloves, finely chopped

1 small chilli, finely chopped (See Tip)

1cm/½ in piece fresh root ginger, thinly sliced

450g creamed or pulped tomatoes

400g can tuna fish in oil, drained and roughly chopped

3 tbsp finely chopped fresh parsley

sea salt

375g/13oz dried linguine

freshly ground black pepper

1 Heat the oil and gently fry the garlic, chilli and ginger for a few minutes until slightly softened. Add the tomatoes and cook for a few minutes, then stir in the tuna, two tablespoons of the parsley and salt to taste and heat through.

2 Cook the pasta in boiling salted water for 8–10 minutes or until al dente, then drain. Toss with the sauce and serve sprinkled with the remaining parsley and add pepper to taste.

Nutrition notes per serving: *609 Calories, Protein 35g, Carbohydrate 77g, Fat 20g, Saturated fat 3g, Fibre 4g, Added sugar 3g, Salt 1.42g.*

TIP

I once bought some bunches of chillies from New Covent Garden market to decorate my restaurant. I thought they looked very innocent with their green, yellow, orange and red colours. But tasting one of them I discovered that not even in India had I ever tasted anything more lethally pungent and piercing! Be very careful with the use of chilli and remember that the green variety is not any less hot (if buying from a supermarket and in any doubt about their strength, check the packet). Having said all this it's not a bad idea to keep some fresh chillies on a string in the larder as they retain much of their flavour when dried. Take care when preparing fresh chillies – do not rub your eyes or skin after slicing and deseeding them, and wash your hands, the knife and chopping board straight away.

OPEN RAVIOLO WITH FISH

This recipe is very popular in my restaurant and will certainly attract the attention of your guests. You can make the filling with vegetables, meat or fish. This is the fish version. I'm leaving it to your imagination to create the meat or vegetarian alternative. If you wish to make it more colourful try using two different colours of pasta.

Serves 6

1.3kg/3lb mussels, about 48

675g/1½lb fresh pasta dough (page 60)

115g/4oz butter

1 garlic clove, very finely chopped

sea salt and freshly ground black pepper

175g/6oz fresh scallops, cut into 5mm/¼in pieces

175g/6oz fresh salmon, cut into 5mm/¼in pieces

175g/6oz monkfish or any other firm white fish, cut into 5mm/¼in pieces (See Tip)

1 tbsp finely chopped fresh parsley

1½ tbsp finely chopped fresh dill, plus sprigs to garnish

2 tbsp dry white wine

1 egg yolk lightly beaten with ¼ tsp fresh lemon juice (optional)

1 tbsp olive oil

1   Scrub the mussels under cold running water, discarding any that are cracked or open. With a small sharp knife, scrape away the beards. Wash them in several changes of cold water until the water is left clean. Place in a large bowl, cover with cold water and leave to stand for 30 minutes. Drain and discard any with open shells.

2   Place the mussels in a large pan with just enough water to cover the bottom. Cover and shake the pan from time to time over a fairly high heat for about 5 minutes or until all the shells have opened. Discard any that do not open. Drain the mussels and take the meat out of the shells.

3   Divide the pasta dough into three equal-sized balls. Roll each out on a lightly floured surface to make three sheets of pasta, each about 25cm/10in square by 3mm/⅛in thick. Cut each sheet into four squares, then lay the 12 squares on clean tea towels.

4   Heat half the butter and fry the garlic for a few seconds. Add salt, pepper, all the chopped fish and mussel meat, and fry for a few minutes until just cooked. Stir in the parsley, the chopped dill and the wine, and let the alcohol evaporate for 1 minute. If the filling mixture seems a little thin, thicken by beating in the egg yolk and lemon juice mixture.

5   Bring a large pan of salted water to the boil adding the oil. Place the pasta sheets in the water, one at a time, to prevent them sticking and cook for 4 minutes. Melt the remaining butter. Carefully remove the pasta and pat dry on clean tea towels.

6   While still warm, place one pasta square on each of six warmed serving dishes. Divide the fish filling between the six dishes and place in the centre of each square. Use the remaining pasta squares to cover the filling and drizzle over the melted butter. Garnish with the dill sprigs.

Nutrition notes per serving: 484 Calories, Protein 35g, Carbohydrate 59g, Fat 13g, Saturated fat 3g, Fibre 3g, Added sugar 0g, Salt 1.29g.

TIP

Monkfish, a round sea fish with a large ugly head, is native to the Mediterranean and both sides of the Atlantic. Only the tail is eaten and it is sold as fillets. Its firm white flesh has a flavour not unlike lobster and it is at its best from October to January.

ORECCHIONI WITH PIQUANT SAUCE

Serves 4

115g/4oz sun-dried tomatoes

4 anchovy fillets, salted or in oil

3 tbsp coarsely chopped fresh basil

3 tbsp coarsely chopped fresh parsley

10g/¼oz capers, drained

2 garlic cloves, finely chopped

1 small chilli (See Tip, page 24)

25g/1oz pitted black olives

6 tbsp virgin olive oil

350g/12oz dried orecchioni (these are large orecchiette, page 60) or use conchiglioni or any large pasta

55g/2oz freshly grated Pecorino cheese

1 Soak the sun-dried tomatoes in lukewarm water for about 1½ hours until soft and the saltiness has been removed.

2 If using salted anchovies, soak in water for 30 minutes, then dry on kitchen paper and remove any large bones. Drain the tomatoes and purée in a food processor with two tablespoons each of the basil and parsley, the anchovies, capers, garlic, chilli, olives, olive oil and 300ml/½ pint of water, until the mixture is smooth and glossy.

3 Cook the pasta in boiling salted water for 12–14 minutes or until al dente. Meanwhile, gently simmer the tomato mixture in a pan for 5 minutes, adding a little more water if becoming too thick. Drain the pasta and toss with the sauce. Add the Pecorino cheese, mix together well and serve with the remaining basil and parsley sprinkled on top.

Nutrition notes per serving: *558 Calories, Protein 20g, Carbohydrate 68g, Fat 25g, Saturated fat 6g, Fibre 5g, Added sugar 0g, Salt 1.84g.*

BLACK ANGEL'S HAIR WITH SCALLOPS

Serves 4

400g/14oz or 8 large or 16 small fresh scallops

6 tbsp virgin olive oil

1 garlic clove, finely chopped

1 small chilli, finely chopped (See Tip, page 24)

150ml/¼ pint dry white wine

2 tbsp finely chopped fresh parsley

sea salt

375g/13oz black capelli d'angelo (See Tip)

1 If using large scallops, detach the coral and cut the white meat into four slices or use the small scallops whole. Heat the oil and gently fry the garlic, chilli, white scallop meat and the corals for 1 minute. Add the wine, parsley and salt to taste.

2 Cook the pasta in boiling salted water for 2–3 minutes or until al dente, then drain. Add to the scallop mixture and mix well.

Nutrition notes per serving: *583 Calories, Protein 31g, Carbohydrate 70g, Fat 19g, Saturated fat 3g, Fibre 3g, Added sugar 0g, Salt 0.82g.*

TIP

Black angel's hair is a very fine type of pasta, made with the addition of cuttlefish ink to give it its colour and is usually sold in cellophane packets in the best Italian food shops. It is extremely fragile and that is why it is only made in nests. When you buy, check that the strands are intact and that you're not taking home a lot of broken pieces.

SQUARE SPAGHETTI WITH GARLIC AND ANCHOVY

2 whole bulbs garlic, peeled and broken into cloves

300ml/½ pint milk

16 salted anchovy fillets, soaked in water, drained and large bones removed

2 red peppers

1 yellow pepper

85g/3oz butter, roughly chopped

450g/1lb fresh square spaghetti (page 60 and See Tip)

1 Cook the garlic cloves gently in the milk for 30 minutes or until softened.

2 Meanwhile, preheat the grill to hot. Grill the peppers until the skins are black. Cool slightly, peel off the skin, discard the seeds and finely slice. Keep warm.

3 Remove the pan of garlic from the heat, add the anchovies and stir with a spoon until they dissolve. Strain the milk, garlic and anchovies through a metal sieve into a pan. Discard sieve contents, heat the liquid gently and add the butter – just enough to melt the butter. Remove from the heat.

4 Cook the pasta for 3–5 minutes or until al dente. Drain and toss well with the sauce. Serve with the warm pepper slices on top.

Nutrition notes per serving: *678 Calories, Protein 22g, Carbohydrate 97g, Fat 25g, Saturated fat 14g, Fibre 6g, Added sugar 0g, Salt 1.73g.*

TIP

To make the square spaghetti: fold the fresh pasta dough sheet into a wide, flat sausage. Cut the rolled pasta across into very thin strips. Shake out the strips of pasta, then holding the pasta at one end wind it into a nest and leave on a clean tea towel to dry for about 30 minutes. Or you can use dried or fresh spaghetti.

RAVIOLONI WITH FISH

140g/5oz monkfish (See Tip, page 27)

140g/5oz fresh salmon

85g/3oz fresh cooked and peeled prawns, roughly chopped

2 tbsp chopped fresh dill, plus 4 sprigs, to garnish

2 egg yolks

sea salt and freshly ground black pepper

675g/1½lb fresh pasta dough (page 60)

55g/2oz butter

1 sachet saffron powder or pinch of saffron strands

1 Make the filling: poach the monkfish and salmon together in simmering water for 12–15 minutes until cooked. Drain and roughly chop, removing any bones. Stir in the prawns, dill, egg yolks, salt and pepper and mix well.

2 Make the ravioloni: roll out the pasta dough on a lightly floured surface to make two sheets of pasta about 50 x 25cm (20 x 10in) and about 3mm (⅛in) thick.

3 Arrange eight heaped teaspoons of the filling on each pasta sheet, 6cm/2½in apart. Cover with the other sheet of pasta. Press gently with your fingers all round the filling to seal the ravioloni shapes, without air bubbles. Cut the pasta into 7.5cm/3in squares with a pastry wheel and lay the ravioloni on a clean tea towel. Cook in boiling salted water for 5–6 minutes, then drain.

4 Meanwhile, melt the butter, adding the saffron powder. If using saffron strands, pound them to a powder with a pestle and mortar. Serve two ravioloni on each plate with a little butter drizzled on top and garnish with the dill sprigs.

Nutrition notes per serving: *717 Calories, Protein 36g, Carbohydrate 88g, Fat 27g, Saturated fat 11g, Fibre 4g, Added sugar 0g, Salt 2.07g.*

Vegetarian

MALTAGLIATI WITH AUBERGINE SAUCE Ⓥ

Maltagliati means 'badly cut' and describes the irregular pieces of pasta which are cut out of the dough with a pastry wheel or knife. This recipe is a dream, especially for vegetarians.

Serves 4

450g/1lb fresh pasta dough (See Tip and page 60) or 400g/14oz dried pappardelle, cut or broken into irregular pieces

200g/7oz aubergine, peeled

6 tbsp olive oil

1 onion, finely sliced

200g/7oz carrots, cut into large matchsticks 5mm/¼in thick

1 garlic clove, finely chopped

1 tbsp chopped fresh basil

2 tsp chopped fresh rosemary or 1 tsp dried rosemary

100ml/3½fl oz red wine

½ vegetable stock cube

sea salt and freshly ground black pepper

1 tbsp finely chopped fresh parsley

85g/3oz freshly grated Pecorino cheese

1 Make the maltagliati: roll out the pasta dough on a lightly floured surface and cut into large oblongs. Using a plain pastry wheel or knife, cut the dough into irregular shapes. Leave the pasta shapes on a clean tea towel to dry for 30 minutes.

2 Cut the aubergine flesh lengthways into slices, then into large matchsticks 5mm/¼in thick. Heat the olive oil over a high heat, add the onion, aubergine and carrot matchsticks and fry until soft, stirring continuously. Reduce the heat and add the garlic, basil and rosemary and cook for 5 minutes.

3 Pour in the wine and 100ml/3½fl oz of water and add the stock cube. Stir to dissolve, then cook for 1–2 minutes to reduce the liquid. Add salt and pepper to taste and the parsley.

4 Cook the pasta in boiling salted water until al dente, allowing 4–5 minutes for the maltagliati or 5–6 minutes for the pappardelle. Toss the pasta in the sauce and serve sprinkled with Pecorino cheese.

Nutrition notes per serving: *648 Calories, Protein 23g, Carbohydrate 73g, Fat 30g, Saturated fat 8g, Fibre 6g, Added sugar 0g, Salt 1.31g.*

TIP

Making your own pasta dough will probably take you about 30 minutes for the actual preparation, but you will get quicker with practice. If you buy fresh pasta, you are unlikely to find the quality or the freshness that match your own hand-made. You can make enough of your own to store for another day. Cut or break into whatever shapes you want, leave to dry completely on a clean tea towel, then pack it very carefully into an airtight bag or container. The pasta will keep in the fridge for two to three days or in the freezer for a couple of months.

TORTIGLIONI WITH MUSHROOMS AND CHEESE Ⓥ

Serves 4

20g/¾oz dried ceps

6 tbsp olive oil

200g/7oz button mushrooms, finely sliced

200g/7oz ricotta cheese, crumbled

115g/4oz coarsely grated Fontina cheese (See Tip, page 36)

55g/2oz freshly grated Pecorino cheese

3 eggs, lightly beaten

sea salt and freshly ground black pepper

375g/13oz dried tortiglioni (See Tip)

1 Soak the ceps in warm water for 20 minutes. Drain, reserving the soaking water. Squeeze the ceps dry and finely chop.

2 Heat the oil and gently fry the button mushrooms. Add the ceps with two to three tablespoons of the reserved soaking water and cook for 5 minutes. Remove from the heat and gently stir in the ricotta, Fontina and Pecorino cheeses and the beaten eggs. (The eggs should not be cooked but remain liquid at this stage.) Taste and add salt if necessary and pepper.

3 Meanwhile, cook the pasta in boiling salted water for 6–7 minutes or until al dente, then drain. Return the pasta to the pan and mix well with the sauce, so that the egg just starts to thicken with the heat of the pasta.

Nutrition notes per serving: *802 Calories, Protein 35g, Carbohydrate 75g, Fat 42g, Saturated fat 16g, Fibre 4g, Added sugar 0g, Salt 1.41g.*

TIP

Tortiglioni is one of the larger pastas that looks like a twisted, hollow macaroni. Sometimes it goes by other names such as ricciolo, fusilli or eliceh. It is usually good with tomato-based sauces, but I would like you to try this exception. This sauce looks a little untidy but tastes delicious.

CAUTION! This recipe contains lightly cooked eggs.

STRAW AND HAY WITH COURGETTES AND PECORINO Ⓥ

Serves 4

2 tbsp olive oil

55g/2oz butter

1 onion, finely chopped

1 garlic clove, finely chopped

400g/14oz firm courgettes, cut into matchsticks

2 ripe tomatoes, sliced into small segments

5 basil leaves, chopped

225g/8oz each of white and green fresh tagliolini (see page 60)

sea salt and freshly ground black pepper

85g/3oz freshly grated Pecorino cheese

1 Heat the oil and butter and gently fry the onion and garlic until softened. Add the courgettes and tomatoes and fry gently, stirring, until cooked. This takes a good 10–12 minutes. Add the basil.

2 Meanwhile, cook the pasta in boiling salted water for 1 minute or until al dente, then drain. Mix the pasta with the sauce, then add salt and pepper to taste. Serve sprinkled with plenty of Pecorino cheese.

Nutrition notes per serving: *554 Calories, Protein 22g, Carbohydrate 56g, Fat 28g, Saturated fat 13g, Fibre 5g, Added sugar 0g, Salt 1.12g.*

FARFALLE WITH FONTINA AND CEPS ⓥ

Serves 4

200g/7oz fresh ceps or shiitake mushrooms, sliced, or 20g/¾oz dried ceps

85g/3oz butter

1 small onion, finely chopped

400g creamed or pulped tomatoes

6–8 basil leaves, chopped

375g/13oz dried farfalle

200g/7oz Fontina cheese, coarsely grated (See Tip)

sea salt and freshly ground black pepper

85g/3oz freshly grated Parmesan cheese, to serve

1   If using dried ceps, soak in warm water for 20 minutes, then drain. Squeeze dry, then finely chop.

2   Heat the butter and fry the onion until golden. Add the ceps or shiitake mushrooms and fry for 2 minutes. Stir in the tomatoes, add the basil leaves and cook for 5 minutes.

3   Meanwhile, cook the pasta in boiling salted water for 8–9 minutes or until al dente. Add the Fontina cheese to the sauce, with salt and pepper to taste. If necessary, gently heat the cheese through so that it melts before you toss the drained pasta with the sauce. Serve sprinkled with Parmesan cheese.

Nutrition notes per serving: *826 Calories, Protein 36g, Carbohydrate 79g, Fat 43g, Saturated fat 26g, Fibre 4g, Added sugar 3g, Salt 2.63g.*

TIP

Fontina is a semi-soft cheese exclusive to the Val d'Aosta region in the Alps where the herds of cows graze on sweet, alpine grass all summer long. No wonder the result is a deliciously sweet, melting cheese, which is pale cream with a red rind. It is classed as a table cheese, but is also used for cooking. Be sure it is the real version and not an imitation.

BRANDELLI WITH ASPARAGUS SAUCE ⓥ

Serves 4

450g/1lb large asparagus spears, peeled and trimmed

85g/3oz butter

1 large onion, finely sliced

3 tbsp milk

450g/1lb fresh pasta dough (page 60)

85g/3oz finely grated Parmesan cheese

sea salt and freshly ground black pepper

1   Cook the asparagus in boiling water for 15–20 minutes or until tender. Remove from the pan and cut about 5cm/2in off the top and keep warm. Cut the lower part of the stems into 1cm/½in pieces.

2   Heat the butter in a pan and gently fry the onion until just soft. Add the small asparagus pieces and the milk and cook for 5–6 minutes. Mash the asparagus with a fork until the sauce is smooth.

3   Meanwhile, make the brandelli: just tear off 5cm/2in pieces of rolled out dough at random to form uneven pieces. Cook in boiling salted water for 3–4 minutes or until al dente, then drain. Mix with the sauce, add the Parmesan cheese and toss well. Season to taste and serve the asparagus tips as a garnish.

Nutrition notes per serving: *615 Calories, Protein 24g, Carbohydrate 65g, Fat 31g, Saturated fat 17g, Fibre 5g, Added sugar 0g, Salt 1.65g.*

FETTUCCINE VERDI WITH WALNUT SAUCE Ⓥ

Serves 4

1 tbsp fresh white breadcrumbs

140g/5oz walnuts or hazelnuts

1 garlic clove

55g/2oz freshly grated Pecorino cheese

sea salt

1 tbsp chopped fresh marjoram

6 tbsp virgin olive oil

4 tbsp Greek yogurt

450g/1lb fresh green fettuccine (page 60)

freshly ground black pepper

1 Soak the breadcrumbs in water for 10 minutes, then squeeze dry. Immerse the nuts in hot water and try to remove as much of their brown skins as you can. Dry on kitchen paper.

2 Place the breadcrumbs and walnuts in a mortar, together with the garlic, Pecorino, salt and marjoram. Pound the ingredients with a pestle to a fine texture. Transfer to a small bowl. Slowly add the oil, stirring constantly with a spoon. Stir in the yogurt to make a smooth sauce.

3 Meanwhile, cook the pasta in boiling salted water for 5–7 minutes or until al dente. Drain and toss the pasta with the sauce. Serve with plenty of pepper.

Nutrition notes per serving: *754 Calories, Protein 23g, Carbohydrate 55g, Fat 51g, Saturated fat 9g, Fibre 5g, Added sugar 0g, Salt 0.61g*

RAVIOLI WITH SPINACH AND RICOTTA Ⓥ

Serves 4

250g/9oz fresh spinach

140g/5oz ricotta cheese

2 tsp grated nutmeg

sea salt and freshly ground black pepper

2 egg yolks

85g/3oz freshly grated Parmesan cheese

450g/1lb fresh pasta dough (page 60)

85g/3oz unsalted butter

4 sage leaves, finely chopped

1 Make the filling: cook the spinach in a little water, then drain well. Squeeze out the excess moisture and roughly chop, then mix with the ricotta cheese. Stir in the nutmeg, seasoning, egg yolks and 25g/1oz of the Parmesan cheese.

2 Make the ravioli: roll out the dough on a lightly floured surface to give two pasta sheets about 3mm/⅛in thick and both about 37 x 24cm/14½ x 9½in in size.

3 Put heaped teaspoons of the filling on one sheet of pasta, 5cm/2in apart. Cover with the other sheet of pasta. Press gently with your fingers all round the filling to seal the ravioli shapes, without air bubbles. Cut the pasta into squares with a pastry wheel, and lay the ravioli on a clean tea towel.

4 Cook the pasta in boiling salted water for 4–5 minutes. Meanwhile, melt the butter, drain the pasta and mix it with the butter. Scatter with sage and serve with the remaining Parmesan cheese.

Nutrition notes per serving: *806 Calories, Protein 31g, Carbohydrate 90g, Fat 38g, Saturated fat 20g, Fibre 5g, Added sugar 0g, Salt 1.56g.*

TIP

The ravioli in this recipe are square (you can make round ravioli too, called tortelli), and different sizes are called raviolini, ravioli and ravioloni (respectively, from the smallest to the largest.) This dish is delicious with a fresh tomato sauce (page 62).

PENNE WITH CHILLI SAUCE Ⓥ

Serves 4

6 tbsp olive oil

2 garlic cloves, finely chopped

2 red chillies, finely chopped (See Tip, page 24)

400g can chopped tomatoes or 450g creamed or pulped tomatoes

2 tbsp finely chopped fresh parsley

sea salt

375g/13oz dried penne rigate

1 Heat the oil and briefly fry the garlic and the chillies. Add the tomatoes and cook for a few minutes, then add the parsley and salt to taste.

2 Meanwhile, cook the pasta in boiling salted water for 5–6 minutes or until al dente, then drain. Add the pasta to the sauce and toss together.

Nutrition notes per serving: *495 Calories, Protein 13g, Carbohydrate 75g, Fat 18g, Saturated fat 3g, Fibre 4g, Added sugar 0g, Salt 0.38g.*

AGNOLOTTI WITH RICOTTA AND TRUFFLE Ⓥ

Serves 4

300g/10½oz ricotta cheese

1 tbsp each of finely chopped parsley, basil and mint

2 egg yolks

pinch of grated nutmeg

55g/2oz freshly grated Parmesan cheese

sea salt and freshly ground black pepper

450g/1lb fresh pasta dough (page 60)

55g/2oz butter

1 small fresh white or black truffle, very finely sliced (See Tip)

1 Make the filling: mix together the ricotta, parsley, basil, mint, egg yolks, nutmeg, half the Parmesan cheese, salt and pepper.

2 Make the agnolotti: roll out the pasta dough on a lightly floured surface to about 3mm/⅛in thick. Cut the pasta into two sheets of the same size. Put teaspoons of filling on one sheet, 5cm/2in apart. Cover with the other sheet of pasta, press gently with your fingers all round the filling to seal the shapes, without air bubbles. Cut the pasta into squares with a pastry wheel and lay them on a clean tea towel.

3 Cook the pasta in boiling salted water for 4–5 minutes, then drain. Melt the butter and mix with the pasta. Serve sprinkled with the remaining Parmesan cheese and the truffle slices on top.

Nutrition notes per serving: *617 Calories, Protein 26g, Carbohydrate 60g, Fat 32g, Saturated fat 17g, Fibre 3g, Added sugar 0g, Salt 1.23g.*

TIP

I include this rather unusual recipe because, if at all possible, I would like you to have the extraordinary experience of tasting the famous white Alba truffle, or even the rather more mild, black one! As a last resort use one tablespoon of truffle oil instead (from a good Italian delicatessen) and reduce the quantity of butter to 25g/1oz.

Baked dishes

CANNELLONI

It is well known all over the world that cannelloni can be made in thousands of ways. Fillings are made from meat, fish or vegetables, or a mixture. In principle the filling is wrapped in a small sheet of cooked pasta, then baked with a tomato sauce.

Serves 4

25g/1oz dried ceps or 200g/7oz fresh ceps, finely chopped

450g/1lb fresh pasta dough (page 60 and See Tip)

1 tbsp olive oil

55g/2oz butter

1 onion, very finely sliced

400g/14oz lean minced beef

sea salt and freshly ground black pepper

pinch of freshly grated nutmeg

1 egg yolk

2 tbsp finely chopped fresh parsley

1 mozzarella cheese, drained and cut into 8 segments (See Tip, page 51)

1 quantity Tomato sauce (page 62)

85g/3oz freshly grated Parmesan cheese

1   Preheat the oven to 220C/425F/Gas 7. If using dried ceps, soak in warm water for 20 minutes, drain and reserve the soaking liquid. Squeeze dry and finely chop.

2   Make the cannelloni: roll out the pasta dough on a lightly floured surface to make two sheets of pasta, each 25cm/10in square and 3mm/⅛in thick. Cut each sheet into four squares and lay on a clean tea towel.

3   Cook the pasta for 4 minutes, adding the squares one by one to plenty of boiling water containing one tablespoon of oil to prevent them sticking. Carefully remove the pasta, using a slotted spoon and pat dry on a clean tea towel.

4   Make the filling: heat the butter and fry the onion until soft. Add the beef and ceps and fry until the beef is browned. Add salt, pepper and nutmeg to taste and set aside to cool slightly.

5   Stir the egg yolk and parsley into the filling mixture and mix together well. Divide the filling between the pasta squares, spooning it down the middle of each piece.

6   Place a mozzarella segment on top of the filling and roll the pasta squares round the filling to make cannelloni tubes. Place two tablespoons of the tomato sauce in the base of a large, ovenproof dish. Lay the cannelloni, side by side, over the sauce and cover with the remaining sauce. Sprinkle with the Parmesan cheese and bake for 20 minutes until golden.

Nutrition notes per serving: *866 Calories, Protein 52g, Carbohydrate 70g, Fat 44g, Saturated fat 23g, Fibre 4g, Added sugar 0g, Salt 2.36g.*

TIP

You can use dried cannelloni which are ready to be filled but, if you do, allow extra cooking time (see packet for instructions). Many people like to use a white sauce with cheese added to cover the cannelloni before baking, but I find this a little rich so I have not included it here. But if you like, top with a sauce.

VEGETARIAN LASAGNE ⓥ

Various versions of this famous dish exist, according to regional and personal preferences. I created this sumptuous dish to please requests for imaginative pasta dishes without meat.

Serves 6–8

550g/1¼lb fresh pasta verdi (page 60) or 450g/1lb dried green lasagne

1 tbsp olive oil, plus extra for frying

2 quantities Tomato sauce (page 62)

300g/10½oz Fontina cheese, cut into chunks (See Tip, page 36)

115g/4oz freshly grated Parmesan cheese

7 eggs, lightly beaten

sea salt and freshly ground black pepper

FOR THE SPINACH BALLS

1.3kg/3lb fresh spinach

1 egg, lightly beaten

2 tbsp dried breadcrumbs

25g/1oz freshly grated Parmesan cheese

freshly grated nutmeg

FOR THE AUBERGINES AND COURGETTES

2 eggs, lightly beaten

2 large aubergines, cut lengthways into 5mm/¼in slices

115g/4oz plain flour

2 large courgettes, cut lengthways into 5mm/¼in slices

FOR THE MUSHROOMS

300g/10½oz fresh oyster mushrooms or shiitake mushrooms, sliced

1 garlic clove, chopped

1 tbsp chopped fresh parsley

1   Preheat the oven to 190C/375F/Gas 5. Make the lasagne: if using fresh pasta dough, roll out on a lightly floured surface to make a single sheet 3mm/⅛in thick. Cut into rectangles about 10 x 20cm/4 x 8in.

2   Cook the fresh or dried pasta, adding the pieces one by one to boiling salted water with one tablespoon of oil, to prevent the pasta from sticking. Allow 5 minutes for fresh pasta, 8–10 minutes for dried. Carefully remove using a slotted spoon and pat dry on clean tea towels.

3   Make the spinach balls: cook the spinach in a little water until tender, drain well and finely chop. Mix with one tablespoon of beaten egg, the breadcrumbs and 25g/1oz of Parmesan cheese. Add nutmeg, salt and pepper to taste. Using your hands, shape the mixture into walnut-sized balls then fry in hot oil until lightly browned on all sides. Remove and drain on kitchen paper.

4   Prepare the aubergines: place one beaten egg in a dish. Dip the aubergine slices into the flour, then into the beaten egg. Heat enough oil to deep-fry the aubergine until golden. Remove and drain on kitchen paper. Prepare the courgettes in the same way as the aubergine slices and set aside.

5   Prepare the mushrooms: heat one tablespoon of oil in a frying pan, add the mushroom slices and fry briefly. Stir in the garlic and parsley, and add salt and pepper to taste.

6   To assemble: place three to four tablespoons of tomato sauce on the base of a large ovenproof dish. Cover with a layer of pasta. Add a layer each of the mushrooms, courgettes, aubergine slices and spinach balls, then a little Fontina cheese. Top with 3–4 tablespoons of tomato sauce, a generous sprinkling of Parmesan cheese and 3–4 tablespoons of beaten eggs. Starting with a layer of pasta, repeat layering until all the ingredients are used, finishing with a layer of vegetables, a sprinkling of Parmesan and a little tomato sauce. Bake for 25–30 minutes until bubbling and golden, then cut into portions to serve.

Nutrition notes per serving for 6: *1023 Calories, Protein 56g, Carbohydrate 81g, Fat 55g, Saturated fat 25g, Fibre 11g, Added sugar 0g, Salt 3.71g.*

TIP

You need to allow plenty of time for the preparation of this dish. The consolation is the wonderful result that will fully justify your efforts. You can prepare this dish and assemble it up to 24 hours in advance. Cover and keep in the fridge, then uncover and bake when required.

TORTELLINI IN PUFF PASTRY

The idea of putting pasta in a pastry case is to collect all the aromas and to release them all at once in front of guests. One could also say it is a good piece of culinary showmanship! In any case the effect on your guests will be surprise and admiration.

Serves 4

400g/14oz puff pastry, thawed if frozen

40g/1½oz butter, plus extra for greasing

1 shallot, finely chopped

115g/4oz cooked smoked ham, sliced

4 fresh sage leaves

freshly grated nutmeg

400g/14oz fresh, meat-filled tortellini

200ml/7fl oz single cream

85g/3oz freshly grated Parmesan cheese

sea salt and freshly ground black pepper

milk, for glazing

1   Preheat the oven to 220C/425F/Gas 7. Thinly roll out the pastry on a lightly floured surface until it is large enough to cover the back of an oval ovenproof dish approximately 23 x 18cm (9 x 7in) and 7.5cm (3in) deep, plus allow an extra 7.5cm/3in all round. Cut the pastry out around the dish. Re-roll trimmings, if necessary, and cut out a lid slightly larger than the base of the dish.

2   Lightly butter the back of the dish and, with the help of the rolling pin, lay the larger piece of pastry over. Trim the edge to neaten. Lightly butter a baking sheet and place the pastry lid on it. Bake both base and lid for 25–30 minutes until golden. Cool slightly, then remove the pastry base and place in an ovenproof serving dish.

3   Heat the butter in a pan and briefly fry the shallot for 1 minute to soften slightly. Add the ham, sage and nutmeg to taste and fry for 2 minutes, stirring.

4   Meanwhile, cook the pasta for 3 minutes or according to the packet instructions and drain. Add the cream, Parmesan cheese and pasta to the ham mixture and mix together well. Add seasoning to taste. Pour the mixture into the pastry base. Cover tightly with the pastry lid and glaze with milk. Bake for 5 minutes to reheat the pastry, then serve at once.

Nutrition notes per serving: *940 Calories, Protein 34g, Carbohydrate 78g, Fat 57g, Saturated fat 20g, Fibre 1g, Added sugar 0g, Salt 3.81g.*

TIP

Sage is one of five herbs that are all-important in Italian cookery and although I always prefer to use it fresh, I admit that the dried varieties still have a natural aroma when cooked. If you are using dried ground sage, use only ¼–½ teaspoon.

ZITA NEAPOLITAN-STYLE

Ziti, zita or zite is a sort of long tubular noodle for everyday eating, served with just a tomato sauce and perhaps some small cubes of mozzarella cheese. But it is also something we use for grand occasions. Then we create a dish like this one here, which is very rich, you really only need a little bit to be satisfied. This recipe takes some time and patience, but the result makes it worthwhile. Let me show you how my mother taught me to cook it.

Serves 8

FOR THE MEATBALLS

300g/10½oz minced beef

1 garlic clove, finely chopped

1 tbsp chopped fresh parsley

25g/1oz freshly grated Parmesan cheese

2 eggs, lightly beaten

40g/1½oz fresh breadcrumbs, soaked in a little milk for 5 minutes, then squeezed dry

oil for frying

FOR THE SAUCE

4 tbsp olive oil

1 onion, chopped

115g/4oz chicken livers, thawed if frozen (See Tip)

2 x 400g cans chopped tomatoes

5 basil leaves, chopped

sea salt and freshly ground black pepper

FOR THE LAYERS

450g/1lb dried ziti or penne or rigatoni

115g/4oz spicy Neapolitan salami, sliced

350g/12oz Fontina (See Tip, page 36) or good mozzarella cheese (See Tip, page 51)

85g/3oz freshly grated Parmesan cheese

4 eggs, lightly beaten

1   Preheat the oven to 200C/400F/Gas 6. Make the meatballs: mix together the beef, garlic, parsley, Parmesan cheese, eggs and breadcrumbs in a large bowl. Using your hands, shape the mixture into walnut-sized meatballs. Heat a little oil and fry the meatballs in batches for 3 minutes or until browned on all sides. Remove and drain on kitchen paper.

2   Make the sauce: heat the oil and fry the onion until nearly transparent. Add the chicken livers and cook for 3 minutes. Stir in the tomatoes, cover and simmer for 20 minutes over a low heat. Add the basil, salt and pepper and simmer for 10 minutes.

3   Meanwhile, cook the pasta in boiling salted water for 5–7 minutes until al dente, then drain well. Toss with some of the sauce so the pasta is coated.

4   Lightly butter a 20 x 25cm (8 x 10in) and 7.5cm (3in) deep ovenproof baking dish. Spread a layer of sauce in the base of the dish, then add a layer of pasta. Arrange some salami, some of the meatballs and slices of Fontina or mozzarella cheese on top. Cover with more sauce and a sprinkling of Parmesan cheese. Repeat layering until all the ingredients are used. When you reach the final layer of Fontina or mozzarella cheese pour on the beaten eggs, which will bind the pasta together. Finish with a layer of sauce and Parmesan cheese.

5   Bake for 25 minutes, then let stand for 5 minutes before serving.

Nutrition notes per serving: *697 Calories, Protein 43g, Carbohydrate 51g, Fat 37g, Saturated fat 16g, Fibre 3g, Added sugar 0g, Salt 2.3g.*

TIP

Chicken livers are very much part of many Italian sauces. Wash and trim before use and be very careful you do not overcook them as they will become dry and coarse.

PENNE TIMBALES WITH AUBERGINES
AND SMOKED MOZZARELLA CHEESE Ⓥ

In Italy the combination of pasta and vegetables has always been made interesting. No one misses the meat in many dishes and this is a good example. Again, it's a recipe worth cooking for several people.

Serves 6–8

450g/1lb dried penne lisce

40g/1½oz butter, cut into pieces

200g/7oz French beans, fresh or frozen

2 tbsp olive oil

450g/1lb carrots, cut into large matchsticks

2 large aubergines, cut lengthways into 1cm/½in strips

1 garlic clove, finely chopped

pinch of grated nutmeg

sea salt and freshly ground black pepper

2 x 300g/10½oz smoked mozzarella cheeses, cut into strips (See Tip)

400g/14oz ricotta cheese

140g/5oz freshly grated Parmesan cheese

8 eggs, lightly beaten

1 Preheat the oven to 200C/400F/Gas 6. Cook the pasta in boiling salted water for 5–6 minutes or until al dente, then drain well. Mix with the butter and set aside.

2 Cook the beans in boiling water until tender, drain and set aside. Heat the oil and fry the carrot matchsticks until lightly browned on all sides. Add the aubergines to the pan with the garlic and fry until golden. Add a pinch of nutmeg, salt and pepper.

3 Lightly butter a 20 x 25m (8 x 10in) and 7.5 (3in) deep ovenproof baking dish. Cover the base of the dish with a third of the cooked pasta. Top with one-third each of the beans, the carrots and aubergines, then the mozzarella and ricotta cheeses, and sprinkle with Parmesan cheese. Repeat layering twice more, finishing with the Parmesan cheese. Pour on the beaten eggs, which will bind the pasta together, and bake for 30 minutes until bubbling and golden.

Nutrition notes per serving for 6: *993 Calories, Protein 61g, Carbohydrate 68g, Fat 55g, Saturated fat 30g, Fibre 7g, Added sugar 0g, Salt 3.10g.*

TIP

The tastiest mozzarella is that which has been traditionally made from buffalo's milk. It is a soft cheese made by working the curd by hand while it is very hot to obtain a spongy, milky-textured ball. You'll find it sold in a plastic bag or wrapped in waxed paper in its own whey.

Salads

PASTA FOR ALL SEASONS

This is a dish for special occasions, and can be eaten warm or cold. It contains truffle oil, which is a very sophisticated and, unfortunately, expensive item.

Serves 4

140g/5oz shiitake mushrooms

140g/5oz oyster mushrooms

115g/4oz chanterelles

6 tbsp olive oil

1 garlic clove, finely chopped

2 tbsp finely chopped fresh parsley

sea salt and freshly ground black pepper

juice of 1 lemon

300g/10½ oz dried fusilli

140g/5oz smoked ham, cut into small strips

3 tbsp double cream (if eating the dish warm)

2 tbsp truffle oil and/or truffle, finely sliced

1   Wipe the shiitake, oyster and chanterelle mushrooms with a damp cloth and cut away the tough part of the stalk of the shiitake mushrooms. Cut the oyster and shiitake mushrooms into fine strips or use whole if they are small.

2   Heat four tablespoons of the oil and fry the oyster and shiitake mushrooms. Add the chanterelles after a few minutes, then cook for another few minutes. Add the garlic, parsley, salt and pepper and fry for a further few minutes, then add the lemon juice. Mix well and set aside.

3   Cook the pasta for 8–9 minutes or until slightly softer than al dente. Drain and mix in a bowl with the mushroom mixture and ham, and add the cream if eating warm. Sprinkle with truffle oil just before serving. Slices of truffle added to this dish make it very, very special.

Nutrition notes per serving: *569 Calories, Protein 18g, Carbohydrate 58g, Fat 31g, Saturated fat 7g, Fibre 3g, Added sugar 0g, Salt 1.56g.*

TIP

Fresh shiitake and oyster mushrooms are now available everywhere because they are cultivated. There is little point in buying them dried. Chanterelles only grow in the wild and they are in season in the spring. They are very expensive and you can't afford to experiment with them, so I suggest you follow a recipe rather than improvising with them.

PASTA SALAD WITH VEGETABLES Ⓥ

Serves 4

200g/7oz asparagus, trimmed

200g/7oz celeriac, cut into large matchsticks

300g/10½oz dried gomiti, sedanoni or manicotti

6 tbsp virgin olive oil

2 tbsp white wine vinegar

sea salt and freshly ground black pepper

2 very large tomatoes, skinned, seeded and roughly chopped

200g/7oz mozzarella cheese, diced

115g/4oz Pecorino cheese, cut into strips

2 tbsp finely chopped fresh basil

1 Cook the asparagus and celeriac separately in slightly salted, boiling water until tender, allowing about 20 minutes. Drain and leave to cool. Cut the asparagus into 2.5cm/1in pieces.

2 Cook the pasta in boiling salted water for 7 minutes or until slightly softer than al dente. Drain and leave to cool slightly.

3 In a bowl, mix together the oil and vinegar, and season with salt and pepper. Stir in the tomatoes, mozzarella and Pecorino cheeses, celeriac, asparagus and basil. Mix well, add the pasta and stir to combine. Check seasoning and serve cold or slightly warm.

Nutrition notes per serving: *712 Calories, Protein 32g, Carbohydrate 62g, Fat 39g, Saturated fat 15g, Fibre 6g, Added sugar 0g, Salt 1.68g.*

PASTA SALAD WITH FISH

Serves 4

10 anchovy fillets, salted or in oil (See Tip)

300g/10½oz dried farfalle or conchiglie

200g/7oz squid, cleaned and cut into strips

6 tbsp virgin olive oil

juice of 1 lemon

sea salt and freshly ground black pepper

115g/4oz smoked salmon, cut into strips

200g/7oz small cooked and peeled prawns, thawed if frozen

3 tbsp finely snipped fresh chives

3 tbsp finely chopped fresh dill

1 If using salted anchovies, soak in water for 30 minutes. Dry on kitchen paper and remove any large bones, then cut into pieces.

2 Cook the pasta in boiling salted water for 7 minutes or until slightly softer than al dente, then drain well and leave to cool. Cook the squid in boiling salted water for 5 minutes, drain and leave to cool.

3 In a bowl, mix together the oil, lemon juice, salt and pepper. Add the cooked squid, anchovies, smoked salmon, prawns, chives and dill, and mix well. Add the pasta, stir well and taste again for seasoning. Serve cold.

Nutrition notes per serving: *564 Calories, Protein 38g, Carbohydrate 58g, Fat 22g, Saturated fat 3g, Fibre 3g, Added sugar 0g, Salt 4.64g.*

TIP

The best anchovies are whole anchovies preserved in salt from delicatessens. They give the best flavour but if you can't get these use canned, filleted anchovies in oil. Drain before using.

Desserts

PAPPARDELLE WITH POPPY SEEDS ⓥ

If you think of that British favourite, bread and butter pudding, then the idea that pasta can be eaten as a pudding won't seem so remarkable. Pasta, like bread, consists of flour and water. Add sugar and some other interesting ingredients and the unexpected becomes irresistible. From my student times spent in Vienna one of the most memorable desserts was a mohnnudeln or poppy-seed pasta. I made my own adaptation to create this recipe which I believe has Bohemian origins.

Serves 4

25g/1oz black poppy seeds

200g/7oz fresh or dried pappardelle or tagliatelle (See page 60)

85g/3oz unsalted butter

1½ tsp freshly grated nutmeg

1 tsp ground cloves

pinch of freshly ground black pepper

85g/3oz vanilla sugar (See Tip) or caster sugar and vanilla essence to taste

1   Preheat the oven to 220C/425F/Gas 7. Spread the poppy seeds in a shallow tin and roast for 10 minutes. Cook the pasta in a pan of boiling unsalted water until al dente, then drain.

2   Melt the butter and add the poppy seeds, nutmeg, cloves and black pepper. Toss the pasta with the warm spices, then sprinkle with the vanilla sugar. If you are using vanilla essence, add to the pan with the spices.

Nutrition notes per serving: *459 Calories, Protein 8g, Carbohydrate 62g, Fat 22g, Saturated fat 11g, Fibre 2g, Added sugar 22g, Salt 0.03g.*

TIP

To make vanilla sugar: place one or two vanilla pods, cut into pieces, into a jar of caster sugar and leave for two to three weeks. You can refill the jar with sugar, using the same vanilla pods for months.

CHOCOLATE PASTA Ⓥ

Serves 4

FOR THE PASTA

250g/9oz plain flour

115g/4oz cocoa powder

25g/1oz caster sugar

pinch of cinnamon

4 eggs

½ tsp vanilla essence

FOR THE SAUCE

6 tsp clear honey

6 tbsp chopped pistachio nuts

1 Sift the flour with the cocoa powder and stir in the sugar and cinnamon. Make a well in the centre of the dry ingredients and add the eggs and vanilla essence, then mix into a smooth dough.

2 Roll out on a lightly floured surface until 3mm/⅛in thick. With a pastry wheel, cut the dough into 2cm/¾in wide by 18cm/7in long strips. (Or use a pasta rolling machine to roll and cut the dough into ribbons.)

3 Cook the pasta in unsalted boiling water for 3 minutes, then drain well and divide between 4 warmed plates. Over each serving drizzle a generous teaspoon of the honey and sprinkle with one tablespoon of the pistachios.

Nutrition notes per serving: *580 Calories, Protein 22g, Carbohydrate 72g, Fat 25g, Saturated fat 7g, Fibre 5g, Added sugar 16g, Salt 0.88g.*

CAUTION! This recipe contains lightly cooked eggs.

SWEET FETTUCCINE

Serves 4

250g/9oz plain flour

55g/2oz butter, cut into pieces

1 egg, beaten

2 tbsp granulated sugar

pinch of sea salt

5 tbsp sweet vermouth

pork lard or dripping for deep frying

sifted icing sugar, to serve

1 Sift the flour into a bowl and rub in the butter until the mixture resembles fine breadcrumbs. Add the egg, sugar, salt and the vermouth. Mix with a round-bladed knife to bring the mixture together, then knead for 5 minutes or until a smooth, fairly stiff dough is formed. Cover and leave the dough to rest in a cool place for at least 2 hours.

2 Make the ribbons: roll out the dough on a lightly floured surface until 3mm/⅛in thick. (Or use a pasta rolling machine to roll the dough.) With a pastry wheel, cut the dough into 2.5cm/1in wide and 20cm/8in long strips. Gently tie the strips into single knots.

3 Heat the lard or dripping in a large, deep pan and when the fat is very hot, deep fry the bows two or three at a time until golden brown. Remove, drain on kitchen paper and leave to cool. Make a mound of bows on a plate and serve sprinkled with icing sugar.

Nutrition notes per serving: *485 Calories, Protein 8g, Carbohydrate 61g, Fat 23g, Saturated fat 12g, Fibre 2g, Added sugar 11g, Salt 0.57g.*

TIP

This dessert is based on an extremely simple pastry, which everyone can make. Its only drawback is that the dough has to rest for a couple of hours so you'll need to plan ahead. We make this pastry all over Italy giving it a different name according to the region, town and even village it comes from.

Basics

FRESH EGG PASTA ⓥ

I think farina 00 flour is the easiest to work with by hand to make fresh pasta dough. The quantity of pasta made below is suitable for making up the recipes in this book. When pasta is cooked until it is al dente, it means it still has some bite to it. But al dente means different things to different people, and you will find it best to taste a piece of pasta regularly as you are cooking it to get it just how you like it.

Makes about 450g/1lb

300g/10½oz durum wheat flour (farina 00), or plain flour, or a mixture of both

3 eggs

pinch of sea salt

1 Sift the flour on to a work surface, forming it into a volcano-shaped mound with a well in the centre. Break the eggs into the well and add the salt. (If you want green pasta, add 85g/3oz well drained, puréed cooked spinach. For red pasta, add 1½ tablespoons tomato purée; for black pasta add 1½ teaspoons of cuttlefish ink.) Gradually draw the flour into the egg mixture until it forms a coarse paste. Add a little more flour if the mixture is too soft or sticky and, with a spatula, scrape up any pieces of dough.

2 Clean your hands and the work surface. Lightly flour the work surface and knead the dough with the heel of one hand, working it for 10–15 minutes until it is smooth and elastic. Wrap in plastic film or foil to rest for 30 minutes.

3 Lightly flour the work surface and a rolling pin. Gently roll the dough out, rotating it in quarter turns, to a sheet 3mm/⅛in thick. After shaping (see below) leave on a clean tea towel to dry for 30 minutes.

For long pasta: Fold the sheet of pasta dough into a wide, flat sausage.
For *pappardelle*, cut the rolled pasta across into 2cm/¾in strips.
For *tagliatelle* also known as *fettuccine*, cut into 5mm/¼in strips.
For *taglierini* also known as *tagliolini*, cut into 3mm/⅛in strips. Shake out the strips of pasta, then holding the pasta at one end wind it into a nest to dry.

For short pasta: Start with a rolled out piece of dough. Divide into two oblongs roughly 12 x 36cm/4 x 16in. Next, divide the two oblongs into neat 6 x 6cm/2 x 2in squares.
For *farfalle*, divide your squares into halves using a serrated pastry wheel. To form the bow or butterfly, pinch the oblong of dough in the centre.
For *orecchiette*, roll out a piece of dough into a sausage, roughly 1cm/½in in diameter and 30cm/12in long. Cut the length of dough into 1cm/½in pieces, then roll to form a ball. Press on the dough ball, at the same time pushing it away from you slightly, so that the dough curls into a shell, or ear shape.
For *cappellacci*, fill 2.5cm/1in squares with your favourite filling, fold into a triangle, pushing out all the air around the filling and pressing the edges to seal. Bring the two widest points of the triangle together, pinching firmly so they hold. Turn the point of the triangle up at an angle to complete the shape.

TOMATO SAUCE

25g/1oz butter or 2 tbsp olive oil

1 onion, finely chopped

400g can chopped tomatoes

6 fresh basil leaves, chopped

sea salt and freshly ground black pepper

1 Heat the butter or oil in a pan and fry the onion until softened. Add the tomatoes and cook gently for 10 minutes. Stir in the basil, season to taste and cook for 5 minutes.

TOMATO AND MEAT RAGOUT

25g/1oz butter or 2 tbsp olive oil

1 onion, finely chopped

280g/10oz lamb, beef or pork on the bone

150ml/¼ pint red wine

2 x 400g cans chopped tomatoes

6 basil leaves, chopped

sea salt and freshly ground black pepper

1 Heat the butter or oil in a heavy-based pan and fry the onion until soft. Add the meat and fry for several minutes until browned. Add the wine and cook for 2–3 minutes.

2 Stir in the tomatoes, cover and simmer very gently for 1½ hours, stirring from time to time. If the sauce becomes too dry add a little water.

3 Add the basil, salt and pepper, and cook uncovered for a further 30 minutes.

CHICKEN STOCK

1.8kg/4lb chicken or chicken pieces

bouquet garni or parsley sprig and bay leaf

1 onion, quartered

3 carrots, quartered

3 celery sticks, with leaves if possible

sea salt and a few black peppercorns

1 Place all the ingredients in a large pan with 3.9 litres/7 pints of water and bring to the boil. Gently skim off the scum as it rises to the surface, using a large flat spoon.

2 Reduce the heat, cover and simmer for at least 2 hours. Remove the chicken, strain the stock and discard the solids. Once cold, remove any solidified fat. It is now ready to be used or frozen for later use.

INDEX

Page numbers in bold refer to photographs

Anchovy 9, 55
  Orecchioni with piquant sauce 28, **29**
  Pasta salad with fish **54**, 55
  Square spaghetti with garlic **30**, 31
Asparagus
  Brandelli with asparagus sauce 36, **37**
  Pasta salad with vegetables **54**, 55
Aubergine
  Maltagliati with aubergine sauce 32, **33**
  Penne timbales with smoked mozzarella **50**, 51
  Vegetarian lasagne 44, **45**
Bacon
  Minestrone 12, **13**
  Pancetta 7, 20
  Speck **9**
Basil 6, **9**
Beef
  Cannelloni **42**, 43
  Pappardelle with meat sauce **18**, 19
  Tomato and meat ragout 62
  Zita Neapolitan-style 48, **49**
Borlotti beans
  Minestrone 12, **13**
Broccoli
  Orecchiette with broccoli **18**, 19
Capers 9
  Orecchioni with piquant sauce 28, **29**
Carrot
  Maltagliati with aubergine sauce 32, **33**
  Penne timbales with aubergines
  and smoked mozzarella **50**, 51
Celeriac
  Pasta salad with vegetables **54**, 55
Cheese 6
  Fontina **9**, 36
    Farfalle with ceps 36, **37**
    Vegetarian lasagne 44, **45**
    Zita Neapolitan-style 48, **49**
  Mozzarella **9**, 51
    Cannelloni **42**, 43
    Pasta salad with vegetables **54**, 55
    Penne timbales with aubergines
    and smoked mozzarella **50**, 51
    Zita Neapolitan-style 48, **49**
  Parmesan 6, **9**
    Penne timbales with aubergines and
    smoked mozzarella **50**, 51
  Pecorino 6, **9**
    Bucatini with bacon, cheese and eggs 20, **21**
    Pasta salad with vegetables **54**, 55
    Straw and hay with courgettes **34**, 35
  Ricotta 6, **9**
    Agnolotti with truffle 40, **41**
    Penne timbales with aubergines and
    smoked mozzarella **50**, 51
    Ravioli with spinach **38**, 39

  Tortiglioni with mushrooms and cheese **34**, 35
Chicken livers
  With tagliatelle 16, **17**
  Zita Neapolitan-style 48, **49**
Chicken stock 62
Chillies 24
  Penne with chilli sauce **2–3**, 40, **41**
Cocoa powder
  Chocolate pasta dessert **58**, 59
Courgettes
  Straw and hay with Pecorino **34**, 35
  Vegetarian lasagne 44, **45**
Eggs
  Bucatini with bacon, cheese and eggs 20, **21**
  Fresh egg pasta 60, **61**
  Penne timbales with aubergines and
  smoked mozzarella **50**, 51
  Vegetarian lasagne 44, **45**
French beans
  Penne timbales with aubergines
  and smoked mozzarella **50**, 51
Garlic
  Square spaghetti with anchovy **30**, 31
Ham
  Cooked
    Pasta with peas **14**, 15
  Parma 7, **9**
    Minestrone 12, **13**
    Taglierini with three mushrooms **22**, 23
  Smoked
    Pasta for all seasons 52, **53**
    Tortellini in puff pastry **46**, 47
Hazelnuts
  Fettuccine verdi with walnut sauce **38**, 39
Luganega sausage
  Penne rigate with sausage 20, **21**
Marjoram 9
Minestrone 12, **13**
Monkfish 27
  Open raviolo with fish **26**, 27
  Ravioloni with fish **30**, 31
Mushrooms 6
  Agaricus bisporus 16
  Cep 6, **9**, 23
    Cannelloni **42**, 43
    Farfalle with Fontina 36, **37**
    Tortiglioni with cheese **34**, 35
  Chanterelle **9**, 23, 52
  Morel 6, **9**, 23
  Oyster **9**, 23, 52
    Vegetarian lasagne 44, **45**
  Pasta salad for all seasons 52, **53**
  Shiitake **9**, 52
    Farfalle with Fontina and ceps 36, **37**
    Vegetarian lasagne 44, **45**
  Tagliatelle verdi with field mushrooms 16, **17**
  Taglierini with three mushrooms **22**, 23
  Tortiglioni with cheese **34**, 35

Mussels
  Open raviolo with fish **26**, 27
Pancetta 7, **9**
  Bucatini with bacon, cheese and eggs 20, **21**
Parma ham 7, **9**
  Minestrone 12, **13**
  Taglierini with three mushrooms **22**, 23
Parsley, flatleaf 9
Pasta 6–7, 32, 35
  Agnolotti with ricotta and truffle 40, **41**
  Black angel's hair **9**, 28
    With scallops 28, **29**
  Brandelli with asparagus sauce 36, **37**
  Bucatini with bacon, cheese and eggs 20, **21**
  Cannelloni **42**, 43
  Chocolate pasta dessert **58**, 59
  Dough 32
  Dried pasta
    Fettuccine **9**
    Orecchiette **9**
    Pappardelle **9**
    Penne lisce **9**
    Penne rigate **9**
    Tagliatelle **9**
    Tubettini **9**
  Farfalle with Fontina and ceps 36, **37**
  Fettuccine verdi with walnut sauce **38**, 39
  Fresh egg pasta 60, **61**
    Angel's hair **9**
    Cappellacci 60, **61**
    Cappelletti **9**
    Farfalle 60, **61**
    Fettuccine **9**, 60, **61**
    Lasagne **9**
    Orecchiette 60, **61**
    Raviolini **9**
    Spaghetti **9**
    Tagliatelle **9**, 60, **61**
    Tagliolini **9**
  Linguine with tuna fish sauce 24, **25**
  Maltagliati with aubergine sauce 32, **33**
  Open raviolo with fish **26**, 27
  Orecchiette with broccoli **18**, 19
  Orecchioni with piquant sauce 28, **29**
  Pappardelle with meat sauce **18**, 19
  Pappardelle with poppy seeds dessert 56, **57**
  Penne rigate with sausage 20, **21**
  Penne timbales with aubergines
  and smoked mozzarella **50**, 51
  Penne with chilli sauce **2–3**, 40, **41**
  Ravioli with spinach and ricotta **38**, 39
  Ravioloni with fish **30**, 31
  Rigatoni with pork ragout **22**, 23
  Salad for all seasons 52, **53**
  Salad with fish **54**, 55
  Salad with vegetables **54**, 55
  Soup with cappelletti **14**, 15
  Square spaghetti with garlic and anchovy **30**, 31

INDEX

Straw and hay with courgettes and
Pecorino **34**, 35
Sweet fettuccine dessert **58**, 59
Tagliatelle verdi with field mushrooms 16, **17**
Tagliatelle with chicken livers 16, **17**
Taglierini with three mushrooms **22**, 23
Tortellini in puff pastry **46**, 47
Tortiglioni with mushrooms and
cheese **34**, 35
Vegetarian lasagne 44, **45**
With peas **14**, 15
Zita Neapolitan-style 48, **49**
Pastry
Tortellini in puff pastry **46**, 47
Peas
With pasta **14**, 15
Pepper 7
Peppers
Square spaghetti with garlic and
anchovy **30**, 31
Pesto sauce 12
Poppy seeds
Pappardelle dessert 56, **57**

Pork
Pappardelle with meat sauce **18**, 19
Penne rigate with sausage 20, **21**
Rigatoni with ragout **22**, 23
Tomato and meat ragout 62
Prawns
Pasta salad with fish **54**, 55
Ravioloni with fish **30**, 31
Sage 47
Salami
Zita Neapolitan-style 48, **49**
Salmon
Open raviolo with fish **26**, 27
Pasta salad with fish **54**, 55
Ravioloni with fish **30**, 31
Smoked
Pasta salad with fish **54**, 55
Salt 7
Sausage
Penne rigate with sausage 20, **21**
Scallops
Open raviolo with fish **26**, 27
With black angel's hair 28, **29**

Speck 9
Orecchiette with broccoli **18**, 19
Tagliatelle verdi with field mushrooms 16, **17**
Spinach
Ravioli with ricotta **38**, 39
Vegetarian lasagne 44, **45**
Squid
Pasta salad with fish **54**, 55
Tomatoes 9
Tomato and meat ragout 62
Tomato sauce 62
Truffles 7, **9**, 40
Agnolotti with ricotta 40, **41**
Pasta for all seasons 52, **53**
Tuna
Linguine with tuna fish sauce 24, **25**
Vanilla sugar 56
Vermouth
Sweet fettuccine dessert **58**, 59
Walnuts
Fettuccine verdi with walnut sauce **38**, 39